Know Thyself

New Insights
for the Divine Process of Opening
Oneself into Enlightenment

By

BILL FOSS

"*If thine eye be single*
Let thy whole body be
Full of Light"

II

Acknowledgements:

I would like to thank everyone who contributed to the book their time, resources and personal support during the last year of constant vigilance in producing this book. Also to all the practitioners, teachers and holy masters who have changed the world for the better with their presence, service and teachings and have made a personal impact on my life and the lives of countless others with continued inspiration for creativity, service, and healing.

All Paintings and Illustrations by Bill Foss
© 2012 Bill Foss All Rights Reserved

ISBN-13: 978-0692572252 (White Wizard Publishing)
ISBN-10: 0692572252

"Know Thyself" new insights & exerps from
"The Secrets of Spiritual Success" First Edition
© 2017 Bill Foss World All Rights Reserved

WHITE
WIZARD

P U B L I S H I N G

Contents

Note: The information and exercises contained within this book are not intended to replace psychological counselling or medical attention. If you feel the need for help, contact a qualified service professional in the appropriate field. Do not attempt to engage in the meditation, visualization, or energy exercises in this book while operating tools, heavy machinery or a motor vehicle.

IV

Dedication

May this Book Serve You as a
Tool and Guide
Into Greater Understanding
Along the Path.
With Eyes that can See
and Ears that can Hear,
"Please God Show Me the Way
of Truth and Light"

Know Thyself

Exerps From

The Secrets of Spiritual Success

Keys to the Art of an Abundant Lifestyle

With new updated insights and information

Introduction

Dear Reader,

It is with gratitude, inspiration, and joy that these writings find you. Through many years of study and self discovery I set out my journey by praying intently one evening, with a feeling in my heart and mind that there was something more. Much more. In my room I quietly asked God to show me the reasons for everything and how it all worked. What followed was a magically synchronistic unfolding of events, ideas and messages that found me first through my art and music, and then through various books and spiritual paths I have continuously studied over the years. I had just started to read *'Life and Teachings of the Masters of the Far East'* a wonderful collection of stories about the masters, the explorers who set out to find them, and the mystical wonders that they incurred. I was instantly astonished, amazed and excited to know that there were such beings operating from the Universal Consciousness of Truth. This followed my asking to be shown the Truth. The inspiration of that moment found me and set me upon what would be a life long trek of connecting with Spirit, realizing it in all things, and expressing it to others through my creativity. Going through the throes of life and the sequence of seemingly mundane events, there were many challenges created by my own thoughts, words and deeds. The dynamic of the contrast between the ordinary moment to moment events of the old ways and patterns sprinkled with the *'aha'* moments of spiritual understanding was a true gift of perception in bringing about a more gradual and constant rhythm of stepping into a more gratifying and loving expression of life. At times even on the spiritual path it was difficult to stay inspired and trusting that all was as it should be, still I ventured forward. What I have found is a deep appreciation not only for God and the realms of Spirit, but also for everything we perceive as mundane and the self induced levels of conflict, separation and loneliness as they would come to be understood as some of my greatest teachers.

This book is a collection of my studies, insights, perceptions and continued asking of Creator God, Great Spirit, Mother Earth and the Earth keepers, Spirit Guides, the Ascended Ones, and all of the many names, ideas and perceptions that have been given to a power greater than ourselves, while witnessing the power and radiance within ourselves in relation to All That Is. May this book serve as a bridge, a window, a doorway into greater understanding for you on your quest for the Truth and a more happy, joyful, peaceful, loving, creative, abundant, thoughtful, inspirational and helpful approach as you journey into your own heart, mind and soul, as you find Your Own True Essence.

William Foss

I feel a stirring in my Soul

Like rain falling on the ocean

A sacred passage

To my heart that's been opened

A sacred flame lights my way

Ever burning

A gentle whisper on the wind

Calling me again

A timeless sage speaking wisdom

Into my Heart

Where no one else can listen.

from Dreaming of Your Love by Bill Foss

Cathedral Rock
Sedona, Arizona
36" x 60" acrylic on canvas

© 2012 Bill Foss

X

I Am the Mother,

Father, Creator

Hallowed is the sacred name

I Am

I Am the kingdom come,

I Am the will being done.

I Am on earth even as

I Am in all kingdoms

from Everlasting by Bill Foss

Know Thyself

PART 1

When you know, not only, who you are in relation to the rest of humanity and in this world, but also as a Divine extension of God and the Universe operating in human form, the playing field becomes much larger and in some ways the rules of the game change. The names and labels become secondary to the Source energy that is now connecting to you and streaming itself through you.

Once connected to Creation in this way, you will never be the same. Your life will become effortless. You will cherish each moment as communion with the Divine through all life and situations. You will have the ability to consider healing yourself and others through prayer and word. You will have the ability to consider manifesting something you may need or desire for yourself or others. You will no longer judge or separate past moments in your life as you are now able to view these moments of contrast as great teachers, else how would you have known? You will heal all past maladies of the mind, body and spirit. All relationships with others will be of compassion and understanding. You will see God operating through the unknown and life's mysteries as well as the known. You will listen and watch for counsel and messages, thoughts, words and deeds. How will life be without conflicts of everyday mundane situations? Is this the 'Peace that Passes All Understanding?' Considerably so.

As you start to awaken, you may have moments of great peace or love, compassion or joyful opening of the heart. These moments of inner silence and elevated higher vibrational emotional states that accompany these moments become noticeable as they start to happen more frequently. One moment of peace, or a heightened state of being is all that is needed for the mind, body, heart and soul in the individual to recognize this state of being and find a moment or passage way back to this state of being. As this starts occurring more often, you may even look forward to these moments with a good feeling or remembrance to the joyful moments which also helps to bring themselves back around. Remember like attracts like.

In this fashion the emotional magnetism of the good feeling moments of being connected will bring more good feeling moments of being connected and then more and then again more, until you recognize that it becomes consistently present more often than not. Still, the moments of emptiness are now recognizable not as the usual constant but as only occasional. And their dynamic is a great indicator or teacher as to what we were once experiencing on a more frequent or moment-to-moment basis. As you come to know yourself, you will come to trust yourself. Your decision making process will become solid. Situations and the process of life will simplify itself for you. You will be able to move through situations quickly that before may have taken weeks, months or years to get past.

Universe Looking Back At Me - Could you imagine a scenario of how limiting it could be to the Universal to see us as reflections and images of God and to see all of the ways in which we are limiting ourselves? The Universe wants to give to us without limit in every moment. Though it often cannot because of the laws of attraction and how we are using them to limit ourselves. So it gives to us incrementally as we can open to the greater possibilities of understanding. Here is an exercise to help you switch your perception:

Close your eyes and relax. Look at yourself as if you were the Universe wanting to give to you and see what you see. You may visualize outer space or expansion of the cosmos, as you look down or over to notice yourself externally. There you are. See who you are. See what your life is like now. Perceive what it is that you would like to add or change and send it to yourself.

Now part 2:

Picture in your mind something you would like to have. Maybe it's a new or different car, or a certain piece of jewelry. Something that will bring you joy.

Once you know what you want, see or visualize yourself standing in the middle of a golden energy field around your body that expands out to create a large glowing bubble around your body. Just outside of your field is that item or object which you would like to acquire.

Now move your consciousness and focus from you in the middle of the golden field over into the object. Become the object and see yourself as the object looking back at you. as you do this, see the golden field of energy coming towards you to engulf you as the object.

Now the original real you comes over to claim the object which you projected into. At this moment your conscious point of awareness is in both places simultaneously and then they merge.

Once you feel you have the item and give thanks for the manifestation come back to the room and open your eyes. You may want to include in your asking: *"...in a clear, easy and safe manner without harm to anything or anyone"*.

Remember the old saying, 'Be careful or full of care in what you wish for'. Many times on the path some have said 'I want it all', and 'I want it now'. What can incur as a result of this may not be balanced and can create more conflict or calamities for a person than anything else.

So take good care in your asking and visualizations and have fun with it! This can be a powerful visualization process. If we can just start and then add to the process or send ourselves things which are most likely to help us in our journey of knowing or understanding ourselves within Creation, and being of service creatively to community and others. The energy and manifestations of the Universe will find us quickly because we and our wishes are in alignment with the goodness. The nature of the Universal Cosmic Energy is good or God. In this way it supports all things we may perceive as dualistic in nature or an element of oneness. As you are visualizing in this way you are:

A. Communicating with God through the Divine Universal Energy.

B. Sharing with God and the Universal what you would like to have or change.

C. Trusting and being watchful as you give it over to God and the Universal Energy to provide what you are asking in the best way for you at this time.

D. Always remember to say 'Thank You" to God, the Universe, the Divine and all the creative agencies involved.

Another aspect of 'knowing yourself' or 'waking up' is that shifts start to occur. In the mind, body, heart, in relationships with others and the world around us and our own lives. As creatures of habit we may see some of these events as threatening to our existence, or our old habitual ways of thinking and doing. Rest assured this is the ego hard at work to keep us in survival mode. Life is always changing. It has been said, *'The only thing that's constant is change.'* It is quite helpful for us to learn to flow and roll with the changes. This can be quite an amazing dynamic. It gives you deeper understanding and deeper meaning to watch and become present to life's 'changing of the guard' as we turn the page and are in the movie's next scene.

As in Tai Chi, we see a situation or opponent coming towards us and with a calm, grounded, centered breath and the inner smile, we yield. Sinking slightly and pivoting on one heel as we slowly shift our weight and move to the side and watch the event or situation move past us in slow motion. The energy being redirected, while our inner chi remains calm centered, gracious and interactively watchful. Then we can go and enjoy some chai tea. When we start to awaken, the inter-personal playing field can shift and change. This is a natural occurrence of the dance or play of different levels of consciousness and how we communicate through them. There are three major scenarios that often occur when people are in relationships together and one person begins their awakening process to know themselves or has become awakened:

1. 'The Enlightened One' convinces 'The Unenlightened One' that the higher path is the way to peace, abundance, joy and all truth and they both can come into alignment together loving, learning together and changing.

2. 'The Enlightened One' practices their new ways of being and tries to convince 'The Unenlightened One' that this is the higher path. 'The Unenlightened One' may reluctantly agree and come along for the ride and merely tolerate all of the lingering divinity.

3. 'The Enlightened One' tries to convince 'The Unenlightened One' that this is the Way, the Truth and the Light, and the 'The Unenlightened One' cannot perceive change, possibly because of traditional religious beliefs, old fashioned family traits or spiralling situations being controlled by the ego from one situational moment to the next becoming layered within the individual whether realized or not. For whatever reason sometimes when one wakes up and the other doesn't, sometimes it just doesn't work out and they move apart or in different directions.

This again, could be God and the Universe at work lining both people up with who they need to be with or what they need to do, learn or experience for the next stage of life's movie or development. Conscious awareness of the situation at hand is needed in order to handle family matters with 'kid gloves'.

Take good care in being present of the other person's needs, thoughts and actions. Perception of the sequence of events and a compassionate view of these dynamics can lend a helping hand and be a great teacher for you as you are coming into who you are, why you are here and who you came here to be. Sometimes when we start the awakening process, we see the dynamics of our surroundings as being out of synchronization with our newly acquired ways of thinking and being. Sometimes this can cause or create varied levels of conflict within ourselves as we see the contrast of our surroundings and the things we want or think we need to change. Be present and ever watchful careful not to inspire a level of hyper-vigilance from within.

This fight-or-flight approach to matters at hand could be more aggravating than helpful and can manifest all nature of additional unwanted red tape with the situation.

In one word, *Balance*. **As within so without. As above so below. Be in the world and not of the world**. This could imply letting Creator step in, or *'Giving it over to God'*. If you are having difficult times at home, pray, asking for God's guidance and messages on a certain situation. Meditate and ask to be shown a mutually agreeable outcome for all parties involved.

There are three levels of perception to consider:

A. God is operating
  'In us, as us and through us'.
B. The Soul is operating
  'In us, as us and through us'.
C. The intellect, our mind using our own brain, is operating
  'In us, as us and through us'.

Mary of Magdala
36" x 48" acrylic on etched copper

© 2012 Bill Foss

These three levels of perception and three states of being are always operating simultaneously through the senses and through the physical human body. At times they shift back and forth and one state of being comes to the forefront of our conscious awareness, while the other levels of being are still accessible and watching, interacting and perceiving the internal and external world. This fundamental understanding could be key in knowing who you truly are as you witness the subtle shifts around this dynamic.

As you become more balanced these three states start operating simultaneously and in a harmonious way, giving you all number of deeper understandings, joy and peace as you move through the world with action and awareness.

To Be In the World and Not of the World. Keep in mind with these precepts that every single person has a different set of circumstances, life path and journey. Like snow flakes we're all individually different. No two are alike, though we're all part of the same snow storm. We all float through the atmosphere together and we all melt when the sun comes out.

So while you're stepping into enlightenment realize that your own recognition of the path could be the same as another's, many others, or very different from anyone. This gives us wings and freedom of perception concerning issues of 'special gifts' that may or may not accompany a higher state of being.

The answers are always right in front of us. We can go as far as we want to go on the path. You may ask yourself, "What is the purpose in doing so?" Different people and beings are at different stages of enlightenment on the path. One person's journey may be that of a teacher, while more intensive levels of study and perception are achieved, adding special understandings or gifts for the purpose of that person's mission. Another may devote themselves to help others in service such as being a healer. Again with certain studies and perceptions of truth, certain understandings, unfoldment of gifts are achieved for aiding that person on their specific mission or life's path journey. Another may come to experience simple joy and peace or... become a leader, builder or farmer? You fill in the blank.

We are all different. Keep this in mind as you study your Life's Path, Soul's Purpose, your Mission in Life or Life's Destiny. We are all different and we attune to Spirit in different ways, some more uniquely and some in a more like-minded fashion. All is being guided and watched over and we have the ability to consciously tune into Spirit and support higher levels of awareness and be actively involved with our surroundings. This is Creator God, Universal Energy, our Soul, our Heart, and our Mind all at work through the physical human expression we call home.

Know Thyself.

Mary Of Sephoris
18" x 24" acrylic on aluminum

This is Creator God,

Universal Energy,

Our Soul,

Our Heart,

and Our Mind

all at work through the

physical human expression

we call home.

Know Thyself.

Know Thyself

PART 2

$\mathcal{A}$ll Souls are moving out across the Seven Super Universes from the Source Light of Creation, and from the Source Light of Creator God of Love. Many Souls coming directly from God in the First Moment of Creation. Other Souls are being created in other star systems or celestial bodies such as stars and star clouds.

Some souls are created by way of an evolutionary process of starlight reaching the earth and combining itself with Earth energy and/or elemental energy and evolving itself into a separate soul with it's own knowing and observing awareness. The self realization process for a naturally created 'earth soul' is similar though unique in vibration to a Celestial Soul with a different set of capabilities for creating on the earth plane and processing awareness. They may know themselves in a slightly different way as all Souls are created to naturally observe and participate in the Divine dance of creation and consciousness.

The Souls from the Great Central Sun or First Moment Creator God have a central command...or 'Instruction'. Their harmonic instruction is to Know Thyself or simply 'know the self'. To come into agreement or knowing with the individual or personal self by observing each personal moment and naturally reporting back to Creator God through direct unified connection and also through the Akashic Records. Reporting, observing, processing and creating continually a series of emotional responses, thoughts, words and actions, neurological responses and creative projections through the senses, brain and the mind field.

So now here we have a new hidden

key to this ancient phrase, Know Thyself.

We are knowing ourselves continually in each and every moment by observing, interacting and responding with all life. Enlightenment is literally hovering right in front of your eyes in every moment... hidden.

Until we perceive things through a new set of lenses, seemingly the same, with continually changing or recurring moments and all of a sudden we see life's moments in a whole new way, or maybe even just a momentary glimpse of a whole new way. If it is a momentary sensation, either way, you will get back eventually to the 'whole new way'.

This process of Self Knowing is the way that Creator unifies or brings the Great Self into the One or completion.

As you start your vibratory 'wake up process' you are not only affecting yourself on multiple levels, as the energy of new observational and aware moments through your mind, emotions, chakras, tissue, nerves, organs, and cells and many other levels:

• You're changing your DNA and healing tendencies and clearing events of stuck energy with your immediate family.

• You are lighting up your soul in a group of 12 souls governed by an over soul. They will feel your knowing light projections as your group subtly interacts.

• Your ancestral lineage on both sides of the family will receive healing and clearing through your natural awakening.

• Everyone you come into contact with in the world will benefit by osmosis from your continuing new vibrations emanating from your body, energy fields and your Soul field.

• Your guides and family members on the other side will be able to receive healing energy, upliftment and connect with you in new ways that will help them in their completion.

For many souls this is a scheduled opening process. For many others it is an option as far as the timing allowing for more experiences and learning. For those of us who choose to take the leads and start our opening to new ways of Knowing ourselves, this can be a true blessing and a game changer, putting the individual and their soul either back on their scheduled coarse of completion or even ahead of the curve bringing new options, preferences and gifts.

When we become a self knowing being it is beyond the delineation of a faithful being or a trusting being. A knowing being has ingrained certain observations and openings of Self, the external world and God in such a way that it cannot cannot reverse the process.

When you 'know' something to be true, real, created, etc. you become solid with the person, place or thing in such a way that it will forever be a new paradigm of being. The subconscious, conscious and super conscious parts of the mind are all in agreement with one another in a way that allows you to use your 'knowing' to create or manifest.

This is who you are now, whatever that self knowing insight is. Wherever you land at that time, with opportunities to stay at that level or to continue on.

So Knowing the Self is not just a stationary model of being, it's a transitory state that is streaming and radiating through you, from you and around you in a continuing series of moments we refer to as the Eternal Now Moment. As your frequencies shift simultaneously, your thought patterns will shift. The focus of your day to day mental movie will shift. Your body can return to perfection, shift and heal itself. While there are so many colorful details to describe to you in so many ways so that you know what is occurring when it is happening to you. And yet your world will also simplify itself: Less or no drama, better diet, better sleep, more joy, better loving relationships with your significant other, family and friends.

More abundance and prosperity. More time and more creativity. Whenever you start your personal wake up program or it is time for you to naturally open to the next level it will be perfect.

So when you're ready....

Know Thyself.

Bring Your Soul Down Into Your Physical Body

Your Soul has all of the perfect knowing, All of the creativity, All of the healing and balance and All of prosperity that you have always searched for. Often we've had reflections or thoughts of a greater version of our own existence or searched for ways to find it. Now here in this meditation and visualization process you can connect with all of that gently and in a balanced way. As your own Divine Celestial Soul comes down into your physical body it will bring you a myriad of inner strength, perfect truth and peace. Your soul is tending itself in through your crown and through your senses every moment you are alive in physical form. When you bring it down into the body consciously it will you perfect knowing and your life will start to line up for you.

While sitting down or standing close your eyes and raise your arms over your head as far as you can, straight up if possible without locking your elbows. If you cannot raise your arms then visualize this in your mind. See a beautiful Golden field of energy over your head or around your body. As you breathe in and out, breathe this golden light into the palms of your hands as you activate it. Feel the energy coming in. As you continue to breathe, once you feel you are connected with this golden field, Your Soul, gently start to slowly bring your hands down in front of or around your body. You are intentionally coaxing your Soul down around and through your body. Bring your hands to rest. Now open your eyes and gently raise your hands and feel the soft liquid field of energy in and around your body. This is You, the Real You.

If you've felt a separation of Self or fragmented, this exercise will bring you back home. Repeat as often as you like.

My Story

Hello, My name is Bill Foss. I was born in a small town in the Midwestern United States in the mid 1960's. From the time of being a small child I had a feeling that something was different. Though I participated in an old fashioned middle class upbringing, there was a creative part of me that felt like I was out of tune with the external surroundings.

I experienced this in my body as an upset stomach or nervousness frequently in response to social interactions and frequently became ill from flus and viruses. There was an invisible question mark over my head and I didn't even know what the question was about. As I continued through my early years I focused inward teaching myself to draw and to express myself through art. Continuing through my high school years I had won a 2 year scholarship to a local junior college hands down out of 500 regional students, though intuitively, I knew it wasn't the right match.

I had already started to learn guitar and played with local bands, sneaking out on school nights to practice my riffs. My plan was to become the best guitarist I could in order to leave and journey out from my small home town. I eventually left in my early 20's touring across the nation for the next 10 years playing on the stage with national touring rock and blues bands.

At age 28, I moved to the southwestern U.S. Landing in New Mexico and playing music locally. I eventually transitioned back into my art by going to art school. There my spiritual process started to open. As I found myself at the end of a 10 year relationship, graduating art school and leaving the music industry all at the same time, I called out to God and Spirit for help and direction.

I began to meet with a new friend who would administer my 1st shamanic soul retrieval. This was not as comfortable as I had hoped as my current and past life karmas had only just begun to unravel. Working locally as a billboard artist for a short time I eventually moved to Arizona for larger art market opportunities.

As I moved deeper into the southwest I started to learn about chi , yoga, and native american spirituality visiting metaphysical stores, spiritual churches and temples searching for deeper meanings. As I prayed very intently from my room one evening before bed, I asked God to show me the way it all worked. To please show me the answers.

The very next day God put me in touch with a book set call "Life and Teachings of the Masters of the Far East" by visiting a used bookstore en route to see an art client. As I read the pages about masters living on the other side of the world doing what we consider to be miraculous things as everyday actions This included bi-location, direct manifesting from the ethers, instantaneous healing, and manipulating the weather and the elements. I knew there was more, I could sense it. I became alive and inspired about life once again.

I had started to become numb or disconnected to the world, not finding through my natural gifts of art and music what I was searching for. While prolific at creating art and music through all the light, sound and color involved with it, I knew there had to be more. I had found the tip of the iceberg. Stories of the Masters of the Himalayas living beyond ordinary reality while deeply connected with God and nature. My spiritual journey had just became a spiritual quest for more knowledge and information as I became even more awake continually to new possibilities and dynamics.

Not long after this in the next 2-3 weeks I asked again for God to please reveal to me more knowledge and information about the way that everything works. I was then guided to a book about the Akashic Records that I read and from which I immediately started absorbing the information. Understanding it all and not knowing how, though I felt like

I already knew this...All of this. At this time in the early 1990's the internet was not developed and not many books out on the subject so it was a challenge to find in depth information on the Akashic Records. So I continued to study and practice accessing my personal Book of Life from within the Akashic Records by way of guided journey meditations that would take me up to the higher

dimensions where the energy was more pure and I could get long range information including veiwing into my past lives. My future path was slowly taking shape.

As I was also studying Tai Chi, Chi Gong and yoga locally, I found my way to a local Self Realization Fellowship temple in central Phoenix that lectured from the Bible and from the ancient Indian Vedas. I witnessed the eastern teachings of Paramahansa Yogananada, a yogi who came to America in the early 1900's from India lecturing about love and God and eventually building centers in the U.S. As I stepped into the bookstore there was a large hard cover book on a stand open to a page with an illustration titled "Babaji, immortal master of the Himalayas."

The next level of my journey had just opened. I had to find out who this was. A few weeks after this I found information about a teacher, Govindan, coming to present Babaji's Kriya Yoga from India. As I took the workshop and learned more about the rights and rituals of

India and the scientific approach and techniques of working with Kriya yoga, I was opened once again to another level of knowledge, teachings and now energy work and meditations.

Continuing on my journey to

understand myself through spirituality, God and metaphysics, next I was guided to connect with and learn about the Ascended Masters through various books and locally meeting spiritual groups. I found a wide array of info on these masters as I kept digging deeper. I was starting to investigate the different levels ascension and the unique information that I found from different masters in different cultures.

As I continued to study the individual lives of various masters I was guided to Sathya Sai Baba, a living master in India who was known for instant manifestations and healings to his followers and in large gatherings of visitors from around the world to his village.

Sai Baba had on several occassions came vividly into my dreams teaching me or bringing gifts. Babaji was also making dream appearances during this time with messages . While all of this was happening I was learning about relationships, creativity, and the everyday throws of life that we all experience. I now had new perspectives which were more important than being caught up or held in lower frequency situations of the inner city workings, as I waded through my long creative process of unfolding

So as I continued my artwork and spiritual studies, upon a friends passing, I was guided to created an 8 foot by 20 foot mural painting on canvas stretchers that showed spiritual masters throughout the ages hovering over the earth. Dr. Joshua David Stone had heard of this painting and invited me to bring the mural to Mt. Shasta, California for a gathering where it was used as the backdrop at the International Wesak festival.

The painting along with a collection of individual ancient masters painted on copper found their way to Europe. Eventually I was called over to Austria to bring more spiritual paintings and to perform at the International Wesak festival in Vienna. It was there that I started some of my very first classes on the Akashic Records. People were eager for knowledge and I found that I had information of value to help others understand the Akashic Records.

Interestingly I had the feeling I was visiting a homeland from past lives. As I continued my spiritual quest I began teaching more and more classes about the Akashic Records. My journeys lead me across the U.S, Europe, the UK and Mexico to teach at spiritual centers and gatherings, bringing my personal blend of learned, practiced and studied techniques as well as insights from past lives and from the teachers on the other side.

In 2011 I started my first book in Sedona Arizona. "The Secrets of Spiritual Success" a collection of higher wisdoms and practical insights gathered over 20 years of my personal experiences with spirituality. I consider the book to be written by the hand of God.

In 2013 I wrote my second book in Austin Texas "Journey to the Akashic Records" a 400 page study book with 2 glossaries originally channelled and compiled in about 3 1/2 months as the Keepers of the Records had been trying

to get my attention for quite sometime to document the existence of the Akashic Records and it's dynamics and whereabouts.

While in Austin I met a living master by the name of Mother Meera. An indian incarnation of the Divine Mother that travels the world healing through 'Darshan' with large groups wherever she goes. Her energy unraveled the blocks in my subtle body and truly helped me to set my feet upon the path of light once more. I have taken time to go see her when she comes to an area and have benefited from her selfless service and healing. Another example of a great living master and what we all may become.

As I continued to teach, I started to give Readings from the Akashic Records for individuals and after several years was eventually guided to start performing healings and energy clearings for individuals as I came to sense and feel through them and around them how to provide them with help. It has been a truly changing and transformative journey as it continues to unfold.

Having been raised Christian in the midwest in a Lutheran church, when I left home early in life I was a rebel and I left the church and my memories of the Sunday services, being an alter boy, and the studies of the Bible, God and Christ behind. Though when in dire straights in the early years sometimes prayer was the only thing I had left. Strangely my prayers were always answered. After a long journey into metaphysics and the New Age I also let my connections with Christ and the Christian side of spirituality fall to the wayside searching for new fresh levels of information.

I experienced a separation between traditional Christianity, which felt old school, and the mystical approach of metaphysics and the New Age movement. As my personal development through the Akashic Records continued, it included memories of past lives in the times of Christ, and that of my own healing processes with which my personal karmas were released. In past years, I've began to become more full circle, not caring if there was a difference between Christianity and any of the other spiritual religions or teachings. I had arrived at the view point, understanding and feelings within myself that it didn't matter anymore. The only thing that matters is peace, love, joy, wellness, being abundantly happy and filled with God's grace and being in reverence of all things within myself and in the world.

As the journey continues to unfold I work with more and more people continually in groups and private readings and healing sessions around the world. I continue to heal, grow and change. And as You step onto the path towards enlightenment and self realization, coming closer to God and finding your true self, may you experience healing, peace and joy and love within yourself and in all ways. God Bless You, I Love You.

International Author, Teacher and Healer Bill Foss guides, teaches and heals through his workshops, books and private sessions. Guided by Spirit through years of studying the Higher Mind, Spiritual Paths from around the world, Ancient Cultures, Healing and the Arts,

Bill brings through today spiritual precepts from ancient times in a clear and concise way to help you unlock the **"Secrets of Spiritual Success"**.

Discover new insights and experiences of the fantastic Akashic Records from the new book "Journey to the Akashic Records". A way station for all souls who have ever come to the earth plane, vastly rich and vivid with information if you know how to get there and use it.

Bill has taught in Austria, the UK, Mexico, and across the US including New York, LA, Dallas, Nashville, Sedona, Phoenix, Seattle, Portland, and Florida, working with groups and individuals.

Learn new insights, energy techniques, life path and past life information, healing and clearing in an Akashic Reading session with Bill as we Journey into the Akashic Records! Bill offers Akashic Records Sessions, Healing and Clearings. Come join Bill for a Workshop or a one to one session and pick up a copy of his Books or CD's and find out about upcoming classes.

WWW.BILLFOSS.NET

SPIRITUAL EVENTS

JOURNEY
TO THE
AKASHIC RECORDS

WITH BILL FOSS

LET YOUR JOURNEY BEGIN FROM WITHIN.

CLASSES
READINGS
WEBINARS

HEALING
PRODUCTS
WORKSHOPS

WWW.BILLFOSS.NET   INFO@BILLFOSS.NET

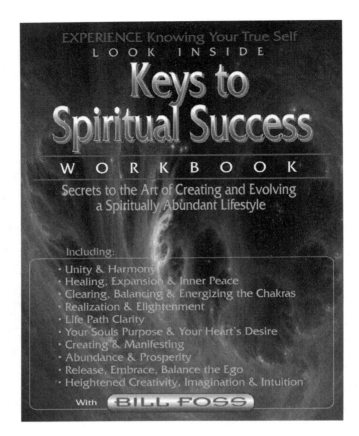

EXPERIENCE Knowing Your True Self
LOOK INSIDE

Keys to Spiritual Success

WORKBOOK

Secrets to the Art of Creating and Evolving
a Spiritually Abundant Lifestyle

Including:

· Unity & Harmony
· Healing, Expansion & Inner Peace
· Clearing, Balancing & Energizing the Chakras
· Realization & Elightenment
· Life Path Clarity
· Your Souls Purpose & Your Heart's Desire
· Creating & Manifesting
· Abundance & Prosperity
· Release, Embrace, Balance the Ego
· Heightened Creativity, Imagination & Intuition

With **BILL FOSS**

"The Keys of Spiritual Success" Workbook, companion to "The Secrets of Spiritual Success" is a collection of creative visualization and healing techniques, energy exercises, meditations, prayers. Exercises and insights to jump start your journey into your own long awaited or continued self inquiry and realization. Use this Workbook to Journal your subtle and not so subtle experiences as you open to greater understandings, fresh ideas, and new ways of being!" Size 8.5" x 11" 165 Pages

Find Your True Creative Self

LOOK INSIDE

Book of Dreams

JOURNAL

DOCUMENT YOUR CREATIVE
IDEAS, THOUGHTS, WORDS
& DREAMS

BILL FOSS

"The "Book Of Dreams" Journal is your gateway into creativity. This is your Journal, your space to create. What will you write, sketch, plan, or invent? Take the opportunity to go within and explore the vast regions, depths, and banks of Divine Creative Potential existing within you, all around you, throughout time, space & beyond. This is your chance to write down, plan and draw out your dream and make it a reality. Use this book as you will to expand your vision. It all starts here, and it starts with you so let's begin. Size 8.5" x 11" 165 Pages

Music &
Meditation
CDs
Available

- **Akashic Healing Angels**(2012) - Guided healing meditation
- **Chakra Music** (2011) - New age meditation music
- **Journey to the Akasha** (2009) - Guided Akashic Records meditations
- **Letting Go into Bliss** -Background music from the workshops
- **Magic of Merlin** (2010) - Akashic Records meditation
- **Super Divine** (2008) - 2 CD set, devotional music, chakra clearing, and Akashic Records meditation
- **Save the Planet** (2003) - New age/rock
- **The Wingmakers** (2005) - New age/rock

Art • Music • Spirit
Products Available
from **Bill Foss** *at* **www.billfossworld.com**

Art - Paintings of the Spiritual Masters or a Personal Soul Portrait on Copper, Brass, or Steel *please see products and examples of originals and commissioned works at the website www.billfossworld.com*

ENERGY HEALING
CHAKRA CHEART

Chakra Charts - Copper or Brass hand made wall hanging 10 in. wide x 7 ft. tall on 7 panels.

NOTES

Made in the USA
Columbia, SC
21 November 2019

83599132R00035